Meet NASA Inventor Stephanie Thomas and Her Team's

Fusion-Powered Spacecraft

www.worldbook.com

Staff

Editorial

Director
Tom Evans

Manager, New Content
Jeff De La Rosa

Writer
William D. Adams

Proofreader/Indexer
Nathalie Strassheim

Graphics and Design

Senior Visual
Communications Designer
Melanie Bender

Media Researcher
Rosalia Bledsoe

Acknowledgments

Cover	© M.Aurelius/ Shutterstock; NASA/Johns Hopkins University Applied Physics Laboratory/Southwest Research Institute; Stephanie Thomas	26-27	© Kletr/Shutterstock
4-7	© Shutterstock	28-33	Stephanie Thomas
8-9	NASA	35	© Princeton Plasma Physics Laboratory
10-11	© Dotted Yeti/Shutterstock	36-37	© Jan Kaliciak, Shutterstock
13	G.Raghav (licensed under CC BY-SA 3.0)	38-44	Stephanie Thomas
14-15	© Sissy Borbely, Shutterstock; © Tim Brown, Science Source		
16-17	© US Dept. of Energy/Science Source		
18-19	© EFDA-JET/Science Source; © TotemArt/ Shutterstock		
21	goffkein.pro/ Shutterstock		
23	© NBC		
25	Stephanie Thomas		

Contents

Glossary There is a glossary of terms on page 45. Terms defined in the glossary are in boldface type that **looks like this** on their first appearance on any spread (two facing pages).

Pronunciations (how to say words) are given in parentheses the first time some difficult words appear in the book. They look like this: pronunciation (pruh NUHN see AY shuhn).

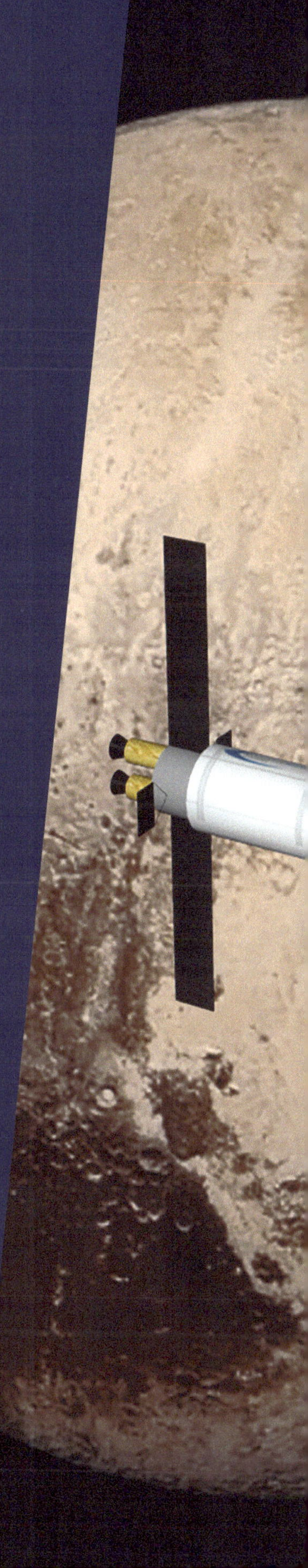

Introduction

Power ranks among our most valuable resources. Here on Earth, power plants generate electric power by burning fossil fuels—such as coal, oil, or natural gas—or splitting **atoms.** Huge **turbines** harness the power of wind and water, and solar panels gather energy from the sun. These facilities and devices produce huge amounts of power to light and heat homes, run businesses, and operate the amazing smartphones, computer networks, and other technology that makes modern life possible.

Out in space, power is even more precious. A space **probe** must carry all the equipment it needs to generate its own power. Some spacecraft rely

on solar panels for electric power. Others rely on batteries or on special **generators** that make use of **radioactive** materials. No matter how a probe gets its power, the amount of power available can limit the probe's ability to maneuver, operate scientific equipment, and communicate with controllers on Earth.

What if there were a way to vastly multiply the amount of power available to a spacecraft? Such a hyperpowered craft could conduct research and maneuver in ways only dreamed of by planners of previous missions.

Inventor Stephanie Thomas and her team are working to develop just such a hyperpowered craft. For a power source, they're looking to harness nuclear **fusion**—the same process that generates the immense power given off by the sun. Thomas's fusion-powered spacecraft would not only enjoy a surplus of energy to run its scientific equipment. It could also use all that power to propel itself in unique ways, exploring farther and faster than ever before.

Meet Stephanie Thomas.

Powering
spacecraft

The sun is an incredible source of energy. In the inner **solar system,** many spacecraft can get the electric power they need just using solar panels. However, sunlight decreases in intensity the farther you get from the sun, making it increasingly difficult to meet a craft's needs using solar power.

The Hubble Space Telescope is powered by two large solar panels.

Engineers have managed to design **probes** bound for Jupiter that rely on solar power. But the farther they get from the sun, spacecraft require ever-larger solar panels to harvest a dwindling amount of power.

Nuclear **fission** reactors are another potential source of power for spacecraft. Such reactors rely on the *fission* (breaking apart) of heavy chemical **elements.** They work in a similar way to nuclear fission power plants on Earth. Fission reactors have been used in a small number of uncrewed spacecraft. Engineers are studying fission reactor designs for use in spacecraft and colonies on the moon and Mars. But, the chemical elements used for fission require careful handling and give off dangerous **radiation.** These elements can also be used to make nuclear weapons, resulting in security concerns. In addition, people worry that these materials could damage the environment if a launch were to fail and the spacecraft came crashing back to Earth.

The most common alternative power source for spacecraft is a device called a radioisotope thermoelectric **generator** (RTG). An RTG makes use of **radioactive** materials, which *decay* (break down) naturally over time, giving off heat. This decay is a form of **fission.** However, an RTG does not involve safety concerns as serious as those of a conventional fission reactor (nor does it produce nearly as much power). It uses a special mix of radioactive elements that decay to provide a

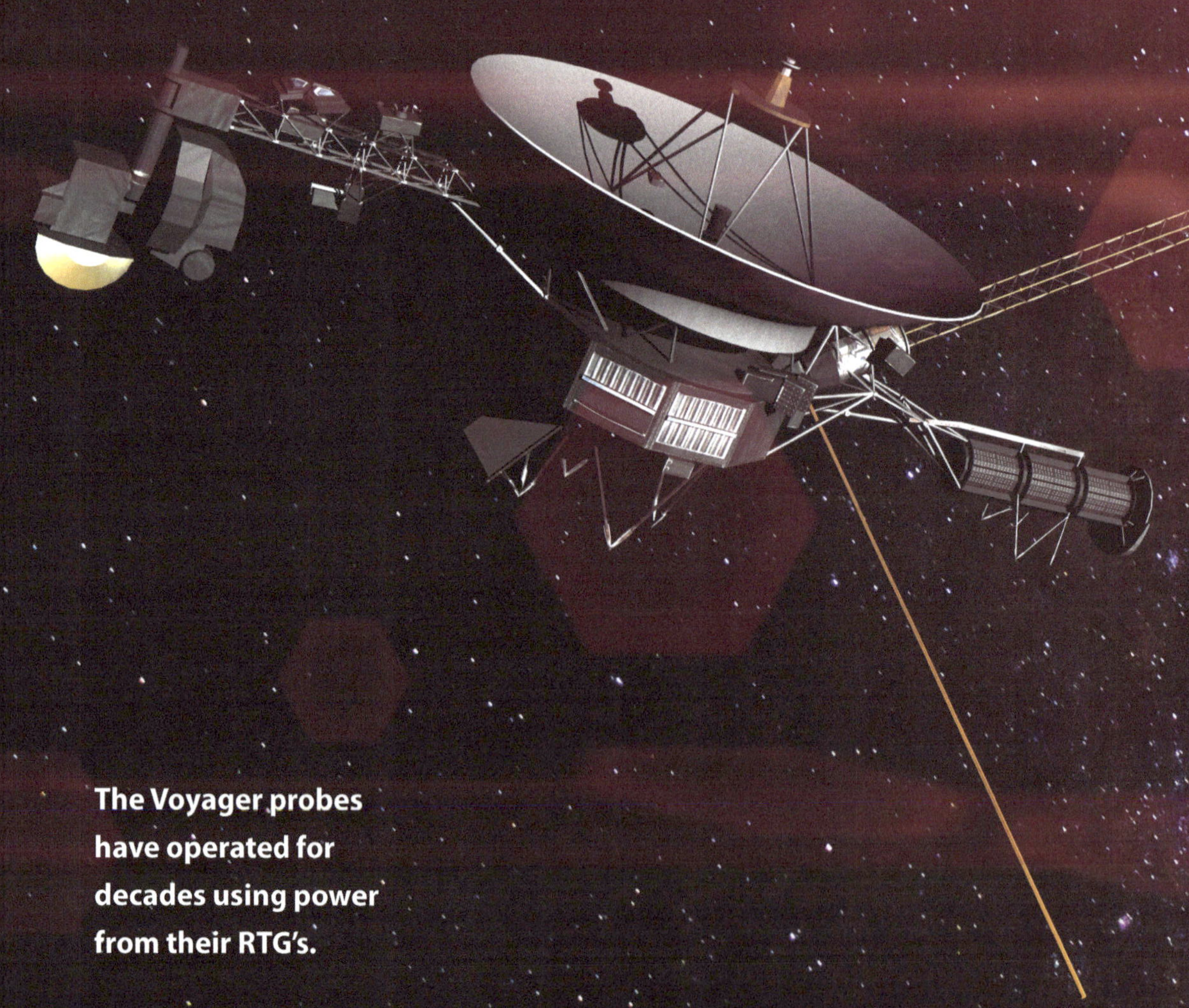

The Voyager probes have operated for decades using power from their RTG's.

steady stream of heat. It then converts this heat directly to electricity. An RTG can produce power for a dozen years or more. The RTG's on the United States Voyager space probes, for example, still generate enough electricity to power a few important instruments and send data back to Earth—over four decades after their 1977 launch.

RTG's aren't a perfect source of power, however. The radioactive materials they rely on are expensive to manufacture and in short supply. Also, as with a conventional fission reactor, people worry that the craft could spread these dangerous materials in the event of a launch failure.

" I'm one of the only people I know of who was interested in **aerospace** at a young age, maintained that interest throughout my schooling, and made a career in aerospace. **"** —Stephanie

Most people change career or chosen profession at least once in life. From an early age, however, Thomas knew exactly what she wanted to be—an aerospace **engineer.** At the time, there were few resources for any children interested in science, technology, engineering, and mathematics (STEM) careers, let alone young girls.

" We didn't have the design or engineering classes offered today, with this focus on STEM. **"** —Stephanie

Thomas did take advantage of the opportunities she had. In high school, she attended a girls' engineering summer program, held at the University of Maryland. In this program, she was able to take a couple of college-level engineering-themed classes. The experience strengthened her interest. She later attended the Massachusetts Institute of Technology (MIT), earning bachelor's and master's degrees in aerospace engineering.

> **I** I picked MIT because it has an aerospace department. There aren't that many schools across the country that have a department exclusively dedicated to aerospace. **II**
> —Stephanie

MIT Department of Aerospace Engineering

To vastly expand the power available to spacecraft, Thomas and her team are working to harness nuclear **fusion**—the energy source that powers the sun itself.

The sun is enormous, holding at least 99.8 percent of the **solar system's mass.** The greater an object's mass, the stronger its **gravitational pull.** The sun's mass has a pull strong enough to hold the entire solar system together. This pull also compresses the sun itself, producing mind-bending extremes of heat and pressure in the sun's interior. These extremes cause the matter there to do something strange.

Most everyday matter is made up of **atoms.** Each atom includes negatively charged particles called *electrons* revolving around a positively charged core called the *nucleus* (plural, *nuclei).* Inside the sun, temperatures

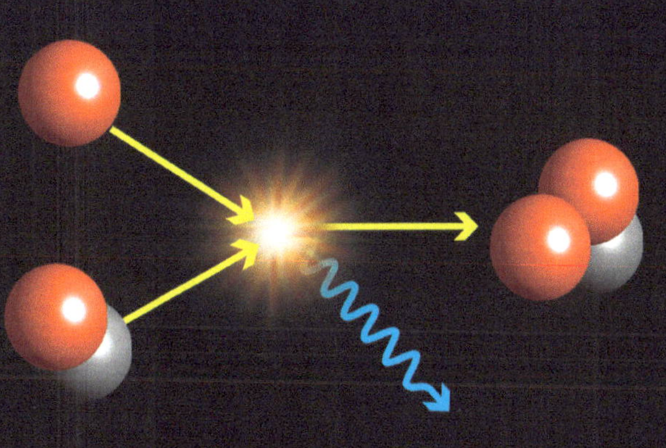

and pressures are so high that nuclei and electrons can move about independent of each other. This state of matter is called **plasma.**

The pressure is so great at the sun's core that the plasma there undergoes fusion. Fusion is the combining of two atomic nuclei to form the nucleus of a heavier **element.** Fusion reactions between lightweight nuclei release a tremendous amount of energy. In the sun's core, hydrogen nuclei fuse into helium nuclei. The resulting energy travels out of the core and eventually radiates out of the sun's surface, bathing the solar system in energy.

If a spacecraft could fuse even a relatively small number of nuclei, it would have a vast power supply to explore the solar system and beyond—no sunlight required!

Fusion on Earth

Fusion power isn't just of interest in spacecraft design. Governments around the world are pouring billions of dollars into research to develop fusion power on Earth. Future fusion power plants might produce extremely cheap, clean, and safe power.

Today's nuclear power plants rely on the **fission** (breaking apart) of heavy chemical **elements.** The materials involved require careful handling and produce dangerous particles even when the reactor is turned off. Fusion reactors produce no dangerous particles when turned off. They also carry no risk of a catastrophic meltdown or other such accident. Spent fuel from fission reactors remains **radioactive** for thousands of years. In contrast, fusion reactors create harmless helium as a byproduct.

Fusion for research is actually happening in machines all around the world. We're just trying to figure out how to do it better. —Stephanie

The promise of **fusion** is too great to ignore. But the difficulties involved are similarly huge.

The sun's enormous **mass** squeezes its core tremendously, holding in atomic nuclei and enabling them to fuse there. Without the benefit of this mass, **engineers** must look for other ways to contain and fuse atomic nuclei. But, temperatures of up to 100,000,000 °C are required to make the nuclei react. Such a high temperature would melt any container. In addition, contact with the container might quickly cool the **plasma** fuel below the necessary temperature. Physicists thus produce controlled fusion with hot plasmas held in place by strong **magnetic fields.**

" In fusion it's all about confinement: how long you can keep the particles around so that they have enough time to get hot and do something useful before they escape. **"** —Stephanie

effective. Cohen modified the shape of the antenna used, changing it from a rectangle or circle to a figure-eight. This simple modification enabled the system to heat the plasma using a fraction of the energy.

Thomas's company, Princeton Satellite Systems (PSS), is working with Cohen to develop a fusion technology called Direct Fusion Drive (DFD). The DFD would not only produce electric power for the craft's instruments but, as the name suggests, it would actually propel the craft as well.

Inventor feature:
Mr. Wizard and sci-fi

Growing up, Thomas was inspired by reruns of a television show called "Watch Mr. Wizard." This educational program aired from 1951 to 1965. It was the creation of the American entertainer Don Herbert, who hosted under the nickname Mr. Wizard. Herbert conducted science experiments using everyday materials, so kids could try them at home. Herbert's friendly demeanor and flashy experiments sparked in many children a lifelong interest in science and **engineering.** "Watch Mr. Wizard" greatly influenced later popular science shows, such as "Bill Nye the Science Guy" (1993-1998) and "Mythbusters" (beginning in 2003).

Thomas was also greatly influenced by science fiction.

> I'm a science fiction buff, and that's because of my dad. My dad's always been interested in science fiction, and our house is sort of a science fiction museum.
>
> —Stephanie

One of her most beloved television shows is "Star Trek: The Next Generation" (1987-1994). The show followed the adventures of the crew of the starship *Enterprise* as it explored the galaxy.

" That was my exposure to space propulsion. I always thought that the engineering guys were so cool on that show, fixing all the problems with the spaceship. They were my people. "

—Stephanie

Big idea:
Combining power and thrust

In the Direct Fusion Drive (DFD), the energy given off by fusion will be used to heat a **propellant.** A propellant is a solid or liquid that is turned into a gas or plasma and pushed out of a rocket, pushing the craft in the opposite direction.

In a conventional rocket, propellant is heated by a chemical reaction. In the DFD, propellant would be fed into the containment area surrounding the fusing **plasma.** The extreme heat produced by fusion would heat the propellant, turning it into a rapidly expanding gas. The pressurized gas would shoot out the back of the containment chamber at high speed, pushing the spacecraft forward.

A DFD prototype.
The copper-colored
RF-heating antennas
can be clearly seen.

The DFD wouldn't be used to launch a **probe** into space. A conventional rocket would launch the probe into orbit around Earth. From there, the DFD would propel the craft to its destination.

Generating electricity

Fusion in the DFD will generate incredible amounts of heat. Thomas and her team are designing a system that would transfer heat away from the fusion reactor and use it to make electricity to power the craft.

Believe it or not, the DFD heat-transfer system will work much like your home air conditioner does. It will use gas to cool the fusion reactor and produce power. The system will be a closed cycle, so none of the gas will need to be vented into space. Cool gas will be compressed and flow around the reactor chamber, absorbing heat. This heated gas will drive a turbine that will create electricity for the radio-frequency (RF) heating system and to power the spacecraft. The gas coming from the turbine will be cooler and lower in pressure since it will have lost energy to drive the turbine. The gas will pass through a radiator to remove the heat that can't be used to produce power. The gas will then be ready to be compressed and sent back toward the reaction chamber.

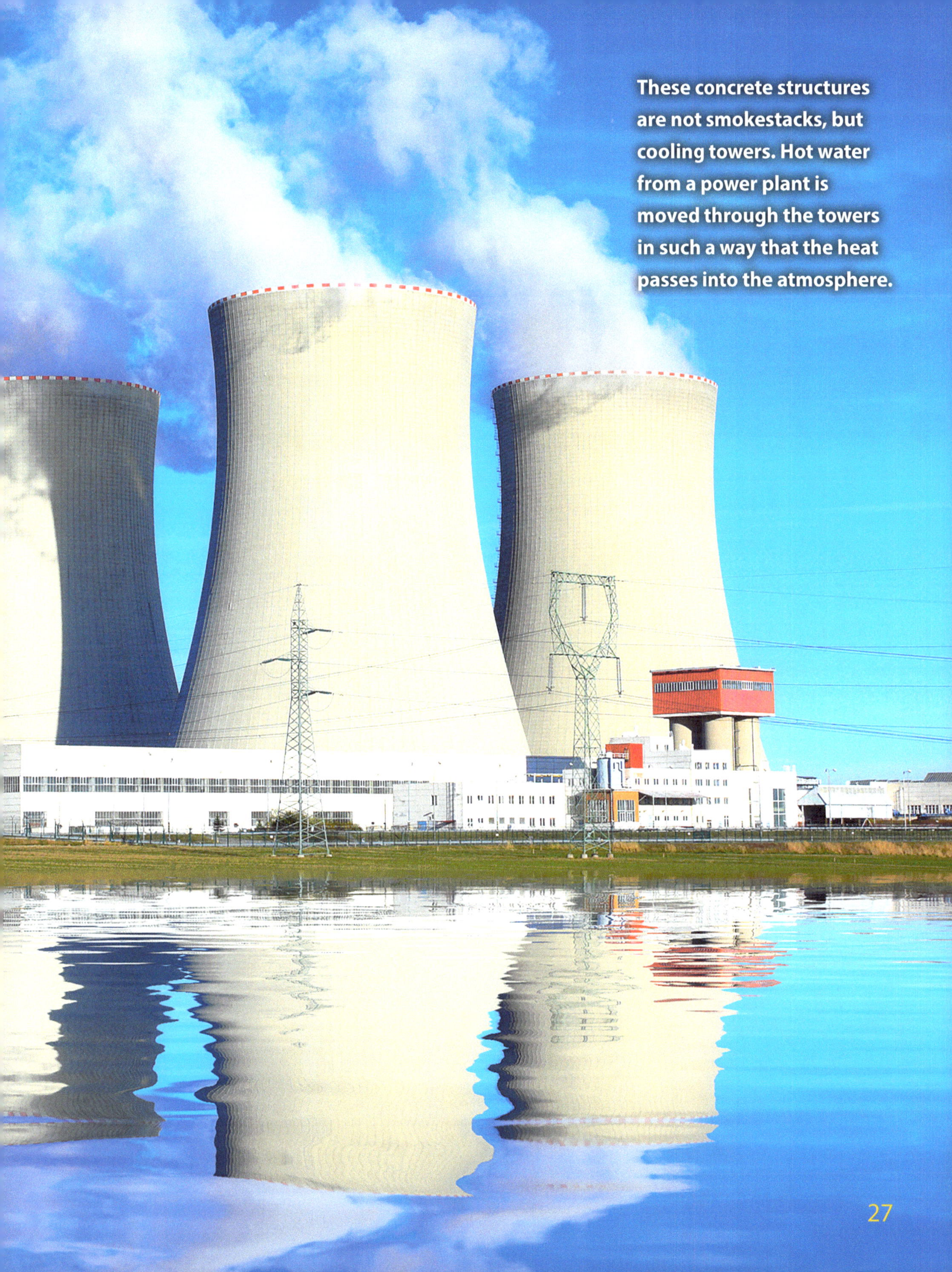

These concrete structures
are not smokestacks, but
cooling towers. Hot water
from a power plant is
moved through the towers
in such a way that the heat
passes into the atmosphere.

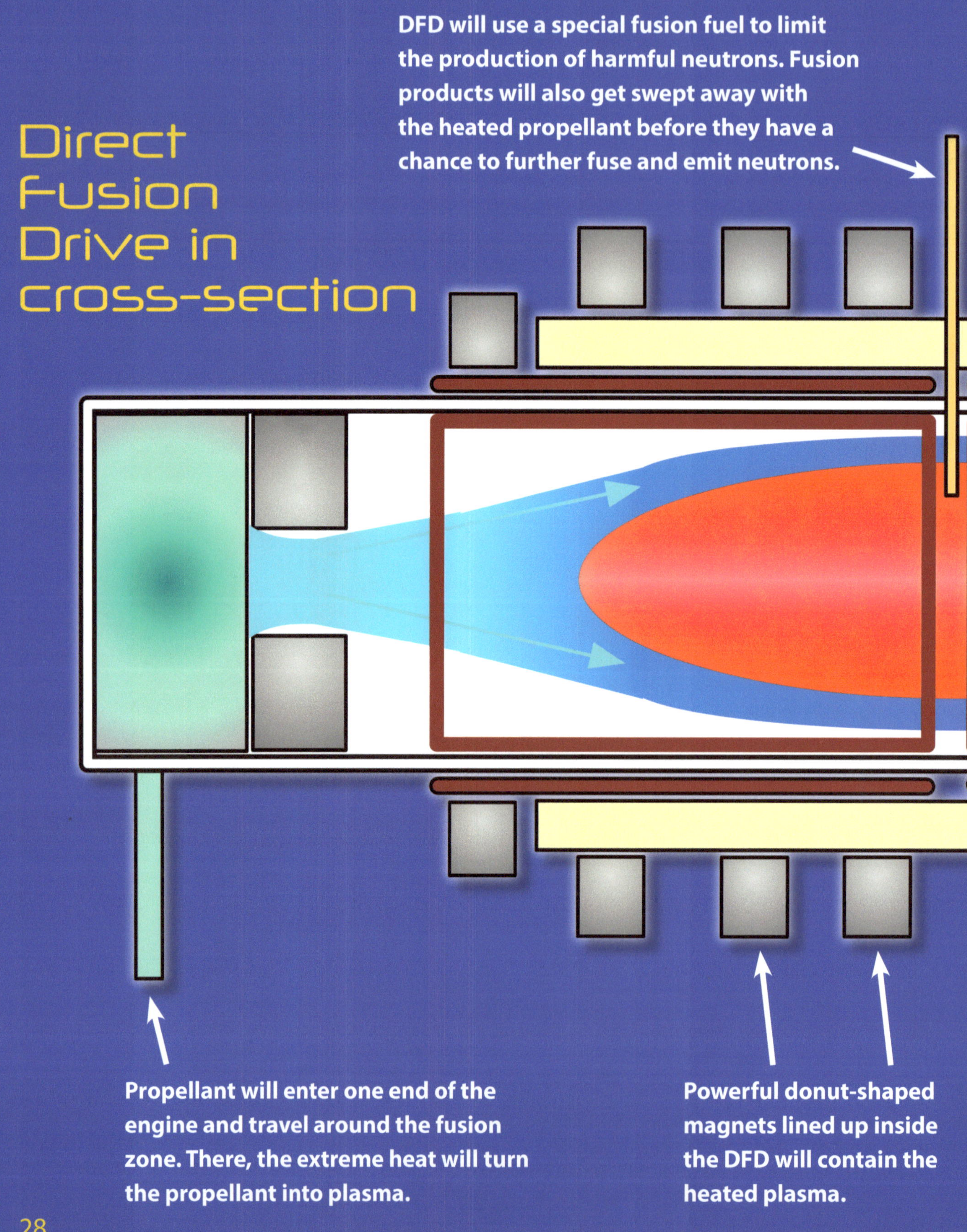

DFD will use a special fusion fuel to limit the production of harmful neutrons. Fusion products will also get swept away with the heated propellant before they have a chance to further fuse and emit neutrons.

Direct Fusion Drive in cross-section

Propellant will enter one end of the engine and travel around the fusion zone. There, the extreme heat will turn the propellant into plasma.

Powerful donut-shaped magnets lined up inside the DFD will contain the heated plasma.

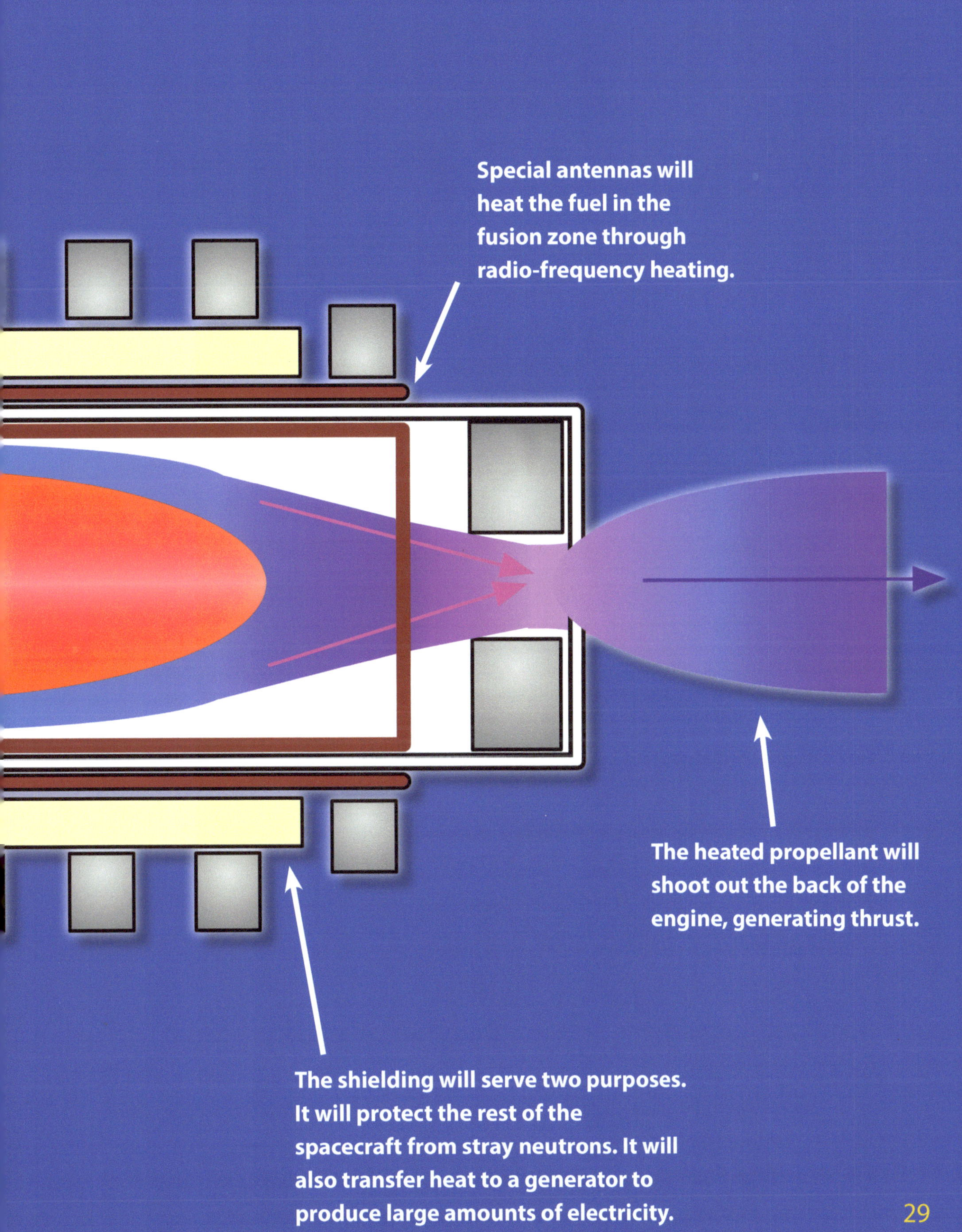

Special antennas will heat the fuel in the fusion zone through radio-frequency heating.

The heated propellant will shoot out the back of the engine, generating thrust.

The shielding will serve two purposes. It will protect the rest of the spacecraft from stray neutrons. It will also transfer heat to a generator to produce large amounts of electricity.

Simple, small, and clean

In developing the DFD, Princeton Satellite Systems has adopted the motto "simple, small, and clean." These qualities serve to distinguish the project from other **fusion** power experiments, such as the International Thermonuclear Experimental Reactor (ITER). ITER, under construction in France, will be vital in the development of workable fusion power plants. But ITER is a huge international undertaking, requiring billions of dollars and decades to complete. By keeping the DFD simple, small, and clean, Princeton hopes to be using it long before ITER is even completed.

Simple. The DFD will make use of radio antennas to heat the **plasma,** rather than the powerful **particle beams** used by ITER and other fusion concepts.

Small. The DFD reactor will be about the size of a minivan, far smaller than most other fusion concepts. In fact, its design only works at smaller scales. ITER, by contrast, will be about the size of a sports stadium. The DFD's small size will allow it to be launched by a single large rocket.

Clean. The DFD will be cleaner than other fusion concepts because it will use a specific fuel mixture to avoid the production of harmful **neutrons.** It will also *exhaust* (release) the products of fusion before they can fuse further, preventing them from releasing harmful neutrons.

Illustration of a ground-
based DFD prototype

Testing DFD

Because the DFD is simple, small, and clean, Princeton Satellite Systems (PSS) can construct **prototypes** more quickly. Through the careful design and testing of prototypes, they can gather valuable information without violating the "clean" part of their motto.

Because some **fusion** reactions generate dangerous **neutrons,** fusion reactors require special shielding and handling. Even though DFD is designed to avoid such reactions, special care will be needed when achieving fusion to ensure safety. PSS's next prototype, PFRC-3, is meant to demonstrate that the DFD can confine and heat **plasma** to high temperatures. However, the prototype will not be able to reach the temperatures needed to fuse the plasma. For this reason, the prototype can be built without special shielding.

Once work with the PFRC-3 is complete, the company will build the prototype PFRC-4. PFRC-4 will be fully shielded to safely demonstrate actual fusion.

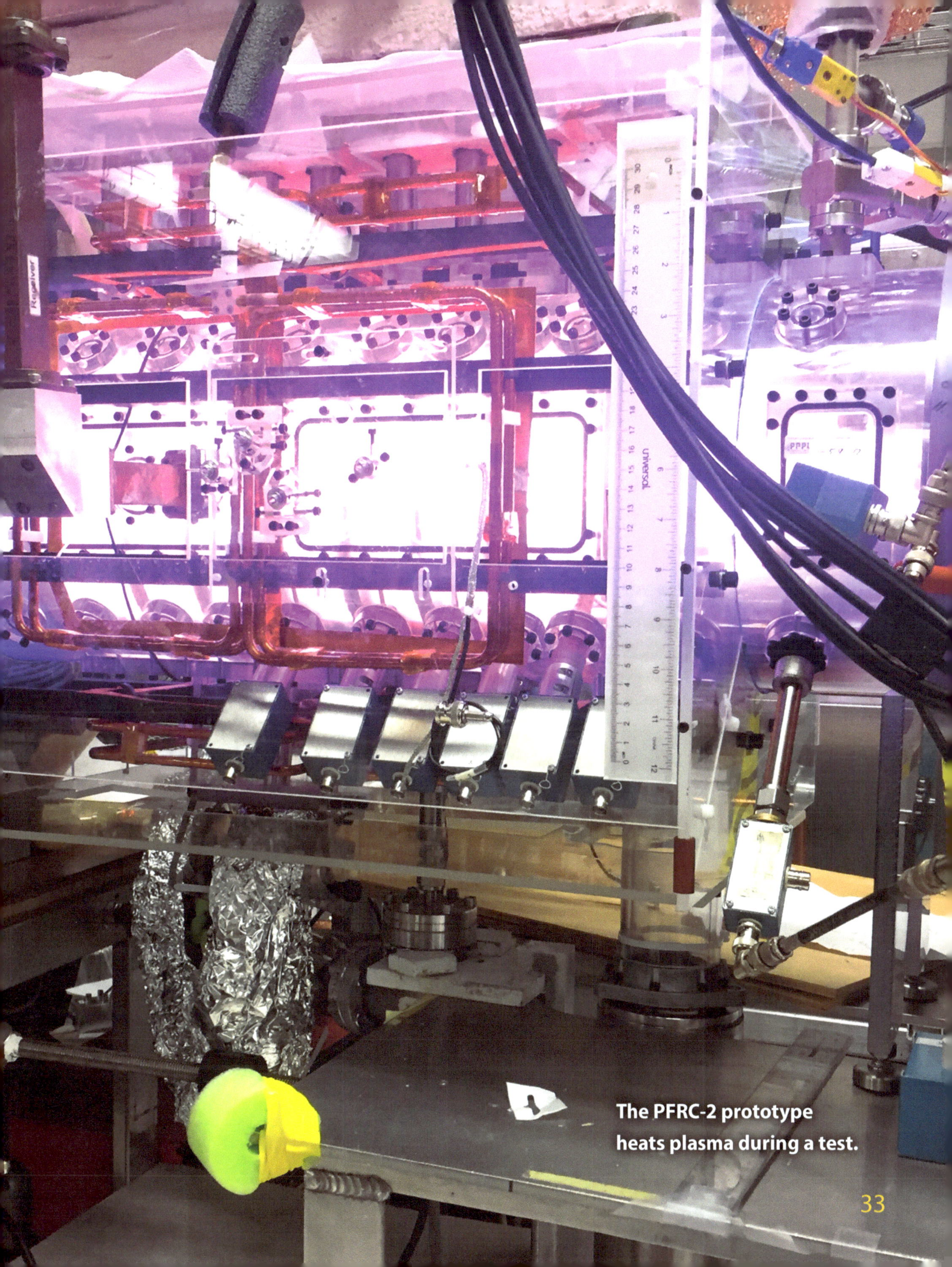

The PFRC-2 prototype heats plasma during a test.

Inventor feature:
The Princeton connection

Thomas happened to grow up near the premier **fusion** research center in the United States. The Princeton **Plasma** Physics Laboratory (PPPL) is a laboratory at Princeton University, in the eastern U.S. state of New Jersey. Many of the most important United States fusion experiments have taken place there. The Tokamak Fusion Test Reactor (TFTR) was built there in the early 1980's. A tokamak is a donut-shaped fusion reactor.

❝ When I was in high school, it used to be front page news in the local newspaper whenever they hit a new temperature. **❞**
—Stephanie

PPPL hosts a winter lecture series called "Science on Saturday." Thomas attended many of the lectures during high school.

❝ It wasn't just on plasma physics. They would have lectures on all different topics. **❞** —Stephanie

Nowadays, much of the U.S. government funding for fusion research goes to the construction of ITER. But PPPL remains a hotbed of fusion research. **Engineers** and physicists are currently repairing and upgrading the laboratory's National Spherical Torus Experiment (NSTX).

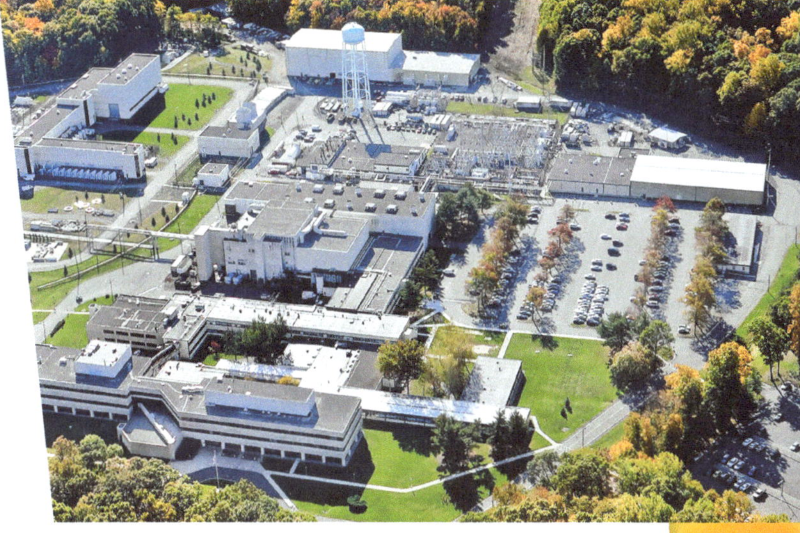

Princeton Plasma Physics Laboratory

❝ I found this small company, which happened to be in my hometown. ❞ —Stephanie

Thomas started at Princeton Satellite Systems (PSS) in 2001. PSS creates software for satellites and satellite control, including navigation, simulation, and data gathering. Thomas had considered going back to graduate school to pursue a Ph.D. degree, but she found she enjoyed working in a small business, where each employee has to cover diverse responsibilities.

❝ In the end, I decided I liked the small business and having to wear a lot of hats (do a lot of different jobs). ❞ —Stephanie

Game-changing power

The DFD will generate a huge amount of electric power. Most space missions have to get by with a few hundred watts. The DFD, on the other hand, will produce 1 to 2 megawatts—almost 10,000 times as much!

This abundance of power will make possible new mission designs. For example, current **probes** use low-power radio transmitters to communicate with Earth, limiting the speed at which they can return data. The DFD will produce so much power that probes could send huge volumes of data back to Earth quickly. A DFD in **orbit** around Mars or another body could use a laser to power a rover on the body's surface. Such a rover would be equipped with special panels—similar to solar panels—tuned to receive **laser** light. When the orbiting DFD probe passes overhead, it would target its laser on these panels, charging up the rover's batteries.

These are just a couple of ideas of how to take advantage of all that power. **Engineers** have long been limited in their design of spacecraft instruments by the electric power available. With this limitation relaxed, they would be free to imagine more powerful instruments to help us learn more about the **solar system.**

In this artist's illustration, a rover receives power beamed down by a satellite orbiting above (not pictured).

Game-changing speed

The DFD will also generate unprecedented propulsion capabilities. Consider NASA's New Horizons **probe,** launched in 2006 to study Pluto and a region of icy bodies called the **Kuiper belt.** The craft was launched at high speed and flew by Jupiter to gain even more speed from the planet's **gravitational pull.** Yet New Horizons took 9 ½ years to reach Pluto, and, when it got there, it shot by the **dwarf planet** at 32,500 miles (52,300 kilometers) per hour, helpless to stop.

Now imagine a similar craft powered by the DFD. Such a probe might fly directly to Pluto in five years, without an assist from Jupiter. Even more tempting, the DFD's ample propulsion could be used to slow the craft, firing in reverse to enter **orbit** around the dwarf planet for an extended stay.

> You're getting there in half the time, but more importantly, you're slowing down and stopping. So it's not a flyby mission, it's an orbiter mission. —Stephanie

A craft with direct **fusion** drive could get to Neptune in four years, Uranus in three years, Saturn in two years, Jupiter in one year, and Mars in four months. With such speed and flexibility, the DFD might "shrink" the **solar system** in much the same way that the advent of air travel was said to shrink the globe.

A DFD-powered probe could enter into orbit around Pluto in only five years.

Down to Earth:

Ideas from space that could serve us on our planet.

The direct **fusion** drive has the potential to be the premier power source for space **probes.** But there is also high demand for clean, reliable power here on Earth.

Most fusion experiments are trying to create a workable power plant—one that would produce power at least as cheaply as do coal and natural gas power plants. The DFD isn't designed to compete with power plants for large-scale electricity production. Its design is such that it would lose much of its efficiency if scaled up.

 —Stephanie

However, the fact that the design is reasonably small and portable lends itself to some mobile applications. For example, DFD-based reactors could be delivered to disaster zones to provide temporary power. The military could use them in installations near the front lines. Isolated communities could even use them to supplement wind or solar power, instead of having to connect to a regional power grid or ship fuel for generators.

Furthermore, discoveries made while testing the DFD could be useful in the design of larger fusion power plants.

Illustration of a DFD-based reactor mounted on a heavy truck. Such a truck could be deployed to provide power to areas affected by natural disasters.

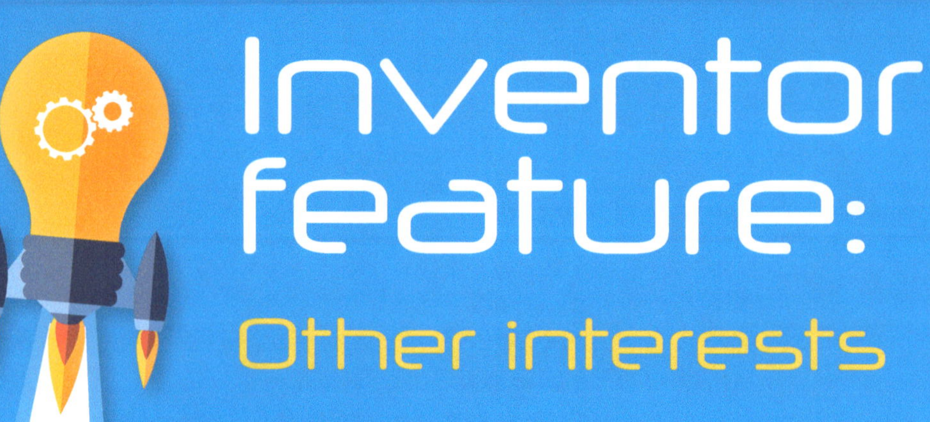

Thomas feeding ducks as a child

Thomas has many interests outside of aerospace. She sings in the Westminster Community Chorus, a choir based out of Rider University in Lawrenceville, New Jersey.

❝ I've always been kind of a naturalist on the side. ❞ —Stephanie

Thomas enjoys nature by hiking and camping with her family, birding, and gardening with native plants.

❝ As a child, I was always out in nature—collecting dragonflies, going out in the creek, and just interested in the wider world. ❞ —Stephanie

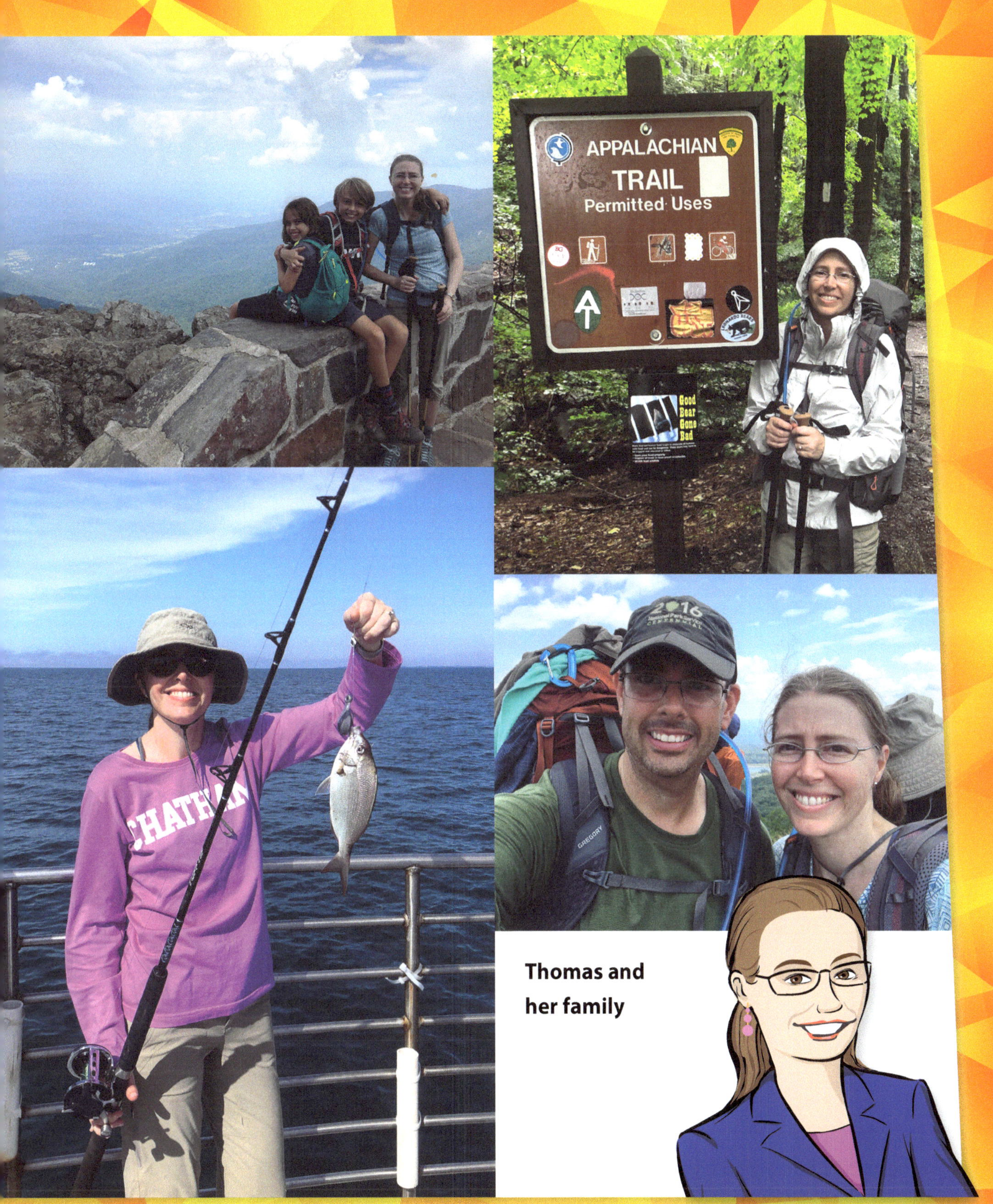

Thomas and her family

Left to right: Dr. Samuel Cohen, Mr. Bruce Berlinger, Dr. Scott Hsu, Mr. Eugene Evans, Ms. Stephanie Thomas, Mr. Michael Paluszek, Dr. Sageeta Vinoth, Mr. Peter Jandovitz

Glossary

aerospace the field of science, technology, and industry dealing with the flight of rockets and spacecraft through the *atmosphere* (the mass of gases that surrounds Earth) or the space beyond it.

atom one of the most basic units of matter, consisting of a *nucleus* (core) of particles called *protons* and *neutrons* with tiny particles called *electrons* moving around the nucleus.

dwarf planet a rounded body orbiting the sun that does not have enough gravitational pull to clear other objects from its orbit.

element a basic unit of matter that contains only one kind of atom.

engineer a person who uses scientific principles to design structures, such as bridges and skyscrapers, machines, and all sorts of products.

fission the splitting of the nucleus of an atom into two nearly equal lighter nuclei.

fusion the combining of two atomic nuclei to form the nucleus of a heavier element.

generator a machine that changes mechanical energy into electricity.

gravitation also called **gravitational pull** or **force of gravity,** the force of attraction that acts between all objects because of their mass. Because of gravitation, an object that is near Earth falls toward the surface of the planet. We experience this force on our bodies as our weight.

Kuiper belt a region of icy objects in the outer solar system, beginning around the orbit of the planet Neptune. The Kuiper belt is also called the Edgeworth-Kuiper belt or the trans-Neptunian disk. An Irish scientist named Kenneth E. Edgeworth suggested in 1943 that the belt existed. The Dutch-born American astronomer Gerard P. Kuiper described it in more detail in 1951.

laser a device that produces a very powerful beam of light.

magnetic field the invisible area of magnetic influence, or effect, surrounding a magnet or magnetic objects.

mass the amount of matter something contains.

neutron a tiny particle with no charge that, together with protons, form the nuclei of almost all atoms.

orbit a looping path around an object in space; the condition of circling a massive object in space under the influence of the object's gravity.

orbiter a spacecraft designed to orbit a planet or other object in space.

particle beam a stream of high-energy atoms or subatomic particles. In some nuclear fusion reactors, neutral particle beams (without a positive or negative charge) are fired into plasma to heat it to fusion temperatures.

plasma a form of matter composed of free (not bound) electrically charged particles. The sun, other stars, and lightning bolts consist of plasma.

probe a rocket, satellite, or other uncrewed spacecraft carrying scientific instruments, to record or report back information about space.

propellant fuel that is turned into gas or plasma and put under pressure to push a spacecraft forward.

prototype a functional experimental model of an invention.

radiation energy given off in the form of waves or tiny particles of matter.

radioactive giving off energy in the form of waves or tiny particles of matter through the breakup of atoms.

rover a lander designed to move about for surface exploration.

solar system the sun and everything that travels around it, including Earth and all the other planets and their moons.

turbine a device turned by the movement of a fluid—for example, the wind—to produce mechanical energy.

Stephanie Thomas and her team developed the Direct Fusion Drive to get large probes to the outer solar system quickly. DFD probes will also have huge amounts of power to use. Your task is to design a mission that will take advantage of the DFD's abilities to learn about the outer solar system. What kind of mission will you develop?

Think about the challenge

Make a list of potential targets in the outer solar system. The possibilities with a DFD-powered mission are virtually endless. Would you go straight to a single target? Would you split time between a planet and its moons? Would you go on a grand tour of the outer solar system like the Voyager probes, before settling into orbit around a distant target? Look up and record what is known about your target or targets and what scientists (and you) would like to find out.

Create your prototype

STEP 2

Now that you've picked a target or targets, it's time to create your probe. Look back on the mission design possibilities enabled by DFD in terms of size and power. After exploring the possibilities and figuring out what fits best for your targets, write out your mission. Model or draw the spacecraft and any other components.

Share your design

STEP 3

Share your design with friends, classmates, or teachers. See what they think could be improved. If possible, share your design with engineers and scientists and ask for their input.

Grow your idea

STEP 4

Remember how Thomas and Princeton Satellite Systems developed a detailed plan of successive prototypes to study the DFD concept in a cost-effective way. Create a similar road map to launch. What do you need to learn to further develop your design? How will you learn it?

Index